Jr. Graphic African-American History

The Middle Passage
and the Revolt
on the Amistad

Susan K. Baumann

PowerKiDS
press

New York

Published in 2014 by The Rosen Publishing Group, Inc.
29 East 21st Street, New York, NY 10010

First Edition

Editor: Joanne Randolph

Book Design: Planman Technologies

Illustrations: Planman Technologies

Library of Congress Cataloging-in-Publication Data

Baumann, Susan K.

The middle passage and the revolt on the Amistad / by Susan K. Baumann. — First Edition.

     pages cm. — (Jr. graphic African-American history)

Includes index.

ISBN 978-1-4777-1311-2 (library binding) — ISBN 978-1-4777-1447-8 (pbk.) — ISBN 978-1-4777-1448-5 (6-pack)

1. Slave trade—America—History—Juvenile literature. 2. Slave trade—Africa—History—Juvenile literature. 3. Amistad (Schooner)—Juvenile literature. 4. Slave insurrections—United States—Juvenile literature. I. Title.

HT1049.B38 2014

306.3'620973—dc23

2013001131

Manufactured in the United States of America

CPSIA Compliance Information: Batch #S13PK1: For Further Information contact Rosen Publishing, New York, New York at 1-800-237-9932

Contents

Introduction 3

Main Characters 3

The Middle Passage and the Revolt on the *Amistad* 4

Timeline 22

Glossary 23

Index and Websites 24

Introduction

Starting in the 1600s, between 10 and 12 million Africans were kidnapped and brought to the Americas to be sold as slaves. Many did not survive the forced march to trading sites in Africa, and many more died during the voyage across the Atlantic Ocean, called the Middle Passage. One group of 53 slaves, who were being sent from Havana to Puerto Principe, Cuba, fought back against their **captors**. They took over the ship, the *Amistad*, and tried to sail back to Africa.

Main Characters

John Quincy Adams (1767–1848) President of the United States from 1825–1829. He **defended** the Africans who had been aboard the *Amistad*.

Cinque (c. 1814–unknown) Leader of the Africans who took over the *Amistad*.

José Ruiz (c. 1815–unknown) Cuban who purchased Cinque along with 48 other Africans who had been taken as slaves.

Lewis Tappan (1788–1873) **Abolitionist** who fought for freedom for the Africans of the *Amistad*.

Martin Van Buren (1782–1862) President of the United States from 1837–1841.

THE MIDDLE PASSAGE AND THE REVOLT ON THE *AMISTAD*

THAT ONE LOOKS HEALTHY. HE SHOULD BE ABLE TO WORK HARD.

SLAVERY HAD A LONG HISTORY IN THE AMERICAS. THE FIRST AFRICAN SLAVES PROBABLY CAME TO THE NEW WORLD IN 1619. FOR NEARLY ANOTHER 250 YEARS, IT WAS LEGAL TO OWN SLAVES IN SOME PARTS OF NORTH AMERICA.

DURING THE 1600S AND THE 1700S, LARGE NUMBERS OF AFRICANS WERE KIDNAPPED. THEY WERE FORCED TO MARCH TO PORTS IN WEST AFRICA WHERE THEY WERE LOADED ONTO SLAVE SHIPS. THEY WERE THEN SHIPPED TO THE AMERICAS AND SOLD INTO A LIFE OF SLAVERY.

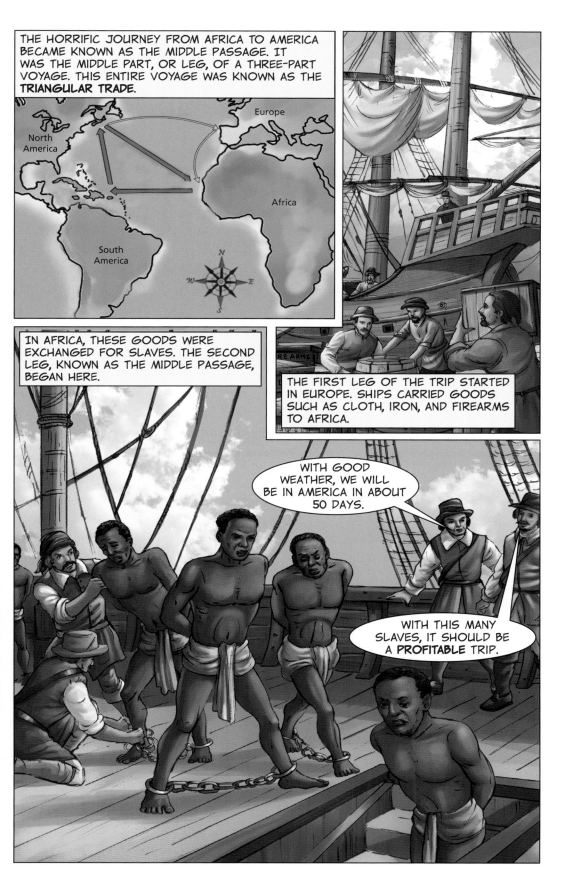

THE HORRIFIC JOURNEY FROM AFRICA TO AMERICA BECAME KNOWN AS THE MIDDLE PASSAGE. IT WAS THE MIDDLE PART, OR LEG, OF A THREE-PART VOYAGE. THIS ENTIRE VOYAGE WAS KNOWN AS THE **TRIANGULAR TRADE.**

Europe

North America

Africa

South America

IN AFRICA, THESE GOODS WERE EXCHANGED FOR SLAVES. THE SECOND LEG, KNOWN AS THE MIDDLE PASSAGE, BEGAN HERE.

THE FIRST LEG OF THE TRIP STARTED IN EUROPE. SHIPS CARRIED GOODS SUCH AS CLOTH, IRON, AND FIREARMS TO AFRICA.

WITH GOOD WEATHER, WE WILL BE IN AMERICA IN ABOUT 50 DAYS.

WITH THIS MANY SLAVES, IT SHOULD BE A **PROFITABLE** TRIP.

IN AMERICA, THE SLAVES WERE SOLD FOR MONEY OR TRADED FOR GOODS SUCH AS SUGAR AND TOBACCO. IN THE THIRD PART OF THE TRIANGULAR TRADE, THE GOODS WERE TAKEN TO EUROPE.

THIS CARGO WILL BRING A LOT OF MONEY IN EUROPE.

CONDITIONS ON SLAVE SHIPS FOR THE MIDDLE PASSAGE WERE HORRIBLE. ABOUT ONE-THIRD OF THE AFRICANS DIED, SOME FROM DISEASE, SOME FROM STARVATION. OTHERS WERE KILLED AS PUNISHMENT.

SOMETIMES SLAVES FOUND A WAY TO FIGHT BACK. ONE WELL-KNOWN REVOLT WAS ON THE SLAVE SHIP NAMED THE *AMISTAD*, BUT THE REVOLT DID NOT OCCUR DURING THE MIDDLE PASSAGE.

THE LEADER OF THIS REVOLT WAS A MAN THE WORLD CAME TO KNOW AS CINQUE. HE LIVED IN MENDELAND. THIS WAS IN WEST AFRICA, A REGION THAT IS NOW PART OF SIERRA LEONE.

WE CAUGHT THIS ONE AS HE WAS WALKING ON A ROAD NEAR HIS VILLAGE.

THE SLAVE TRADERS TOOK CINQUE AND HIS FELLOW CAPTIVES TO AFRICA'S WEST COAST. THE KIDNAPPED AFRICANS WERE KEPT IN LARGE PENS UNTIL THEY WERE LOADED ONTO THE SLAVE SHIPS.

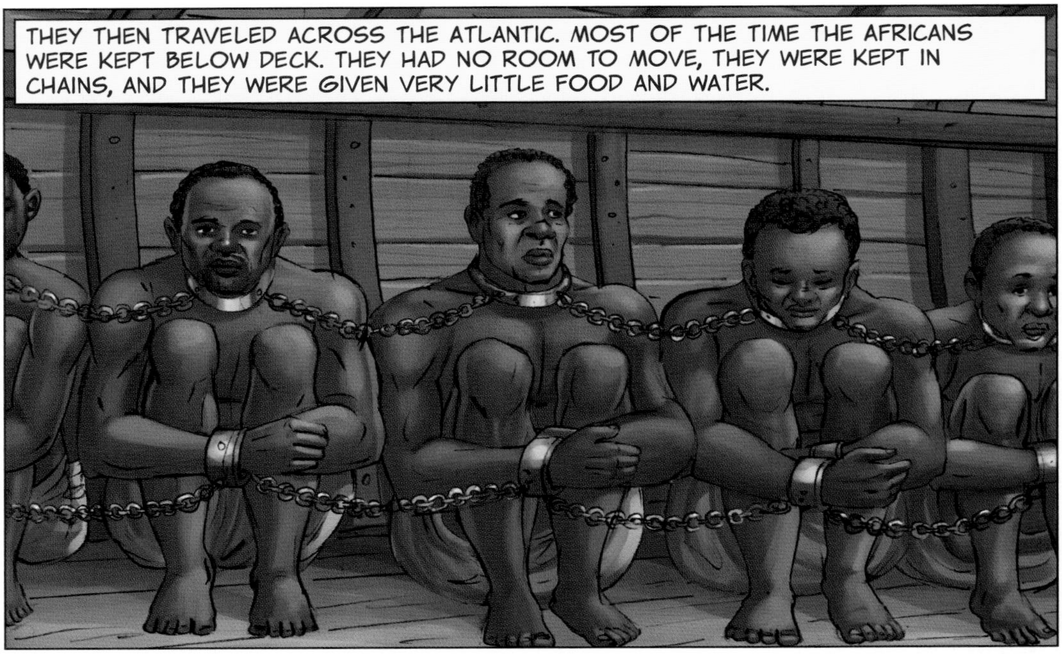
THEY THEN TRAVELED ACROSS THE ATLANTIC. MOST OF THE TIME THE AFRICANS WERE KEPT BELOW DECK. THEY HAD NO ROOM TO MOVE, THEY WERE KEPT IN CHAINS, AND THEY WERE GIVEN VERY LITTLE FOOD AND WATER.

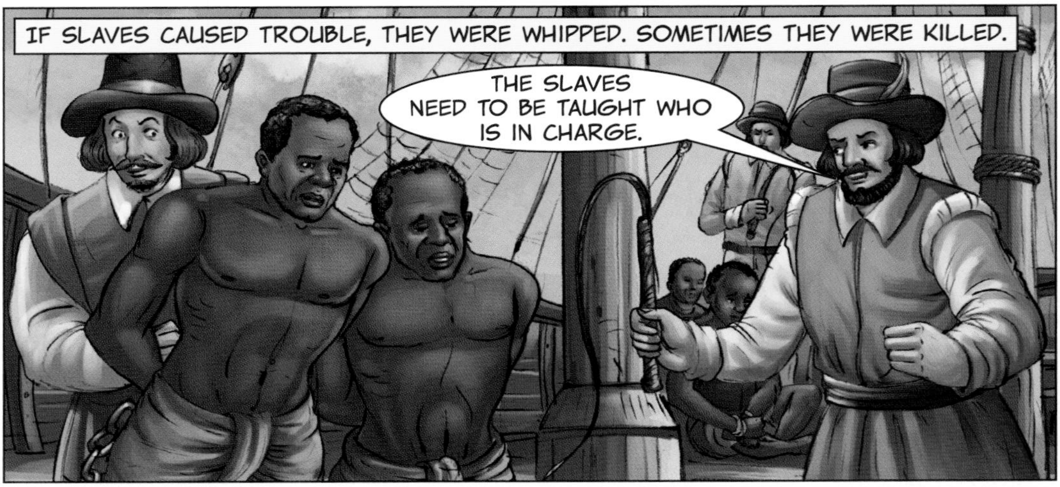
IF SLAVES CAUSED TROUBLE, THEY WERE WHIPPED. SOMETIMES THEY WERE KILLED.
THE SLAVES NEED TO BE TAUGHT WHO IS IN CHARGE.

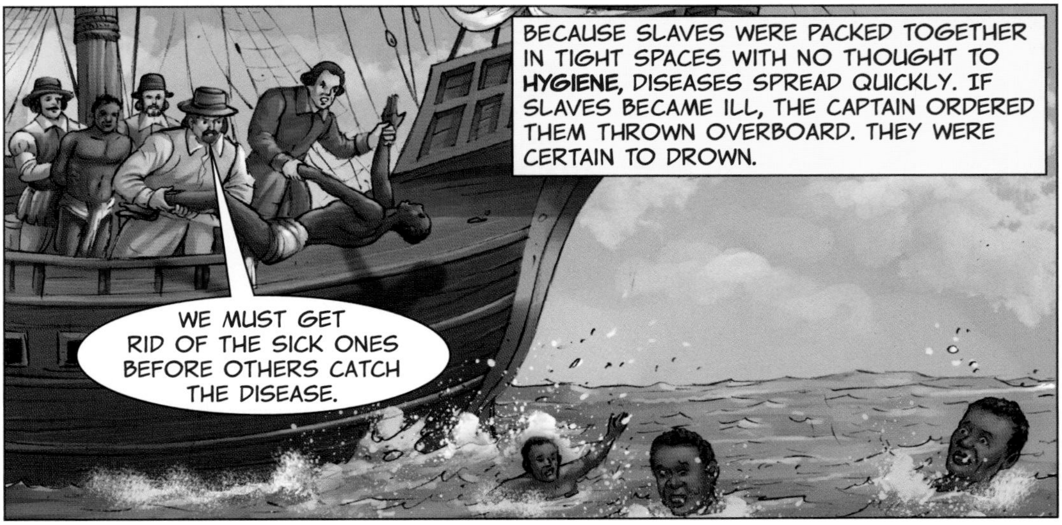
BECAUSE SLAVES WERE PACKED TOGETHER IN TIGHT SPACES WITH NO THOUGHT TO **HYGIENE,** DISEASES SPREAD QUICKLY. IF SLAVES BECAME ILL, THE CAPTAIN ORDERED THEM THROWN OVERBOARD. THEY WERE CERTAIN TO DROWN.
WE MUST GET RID OF THE SICK ONES BEFORE OTHERS CATCH THE DISEASE.

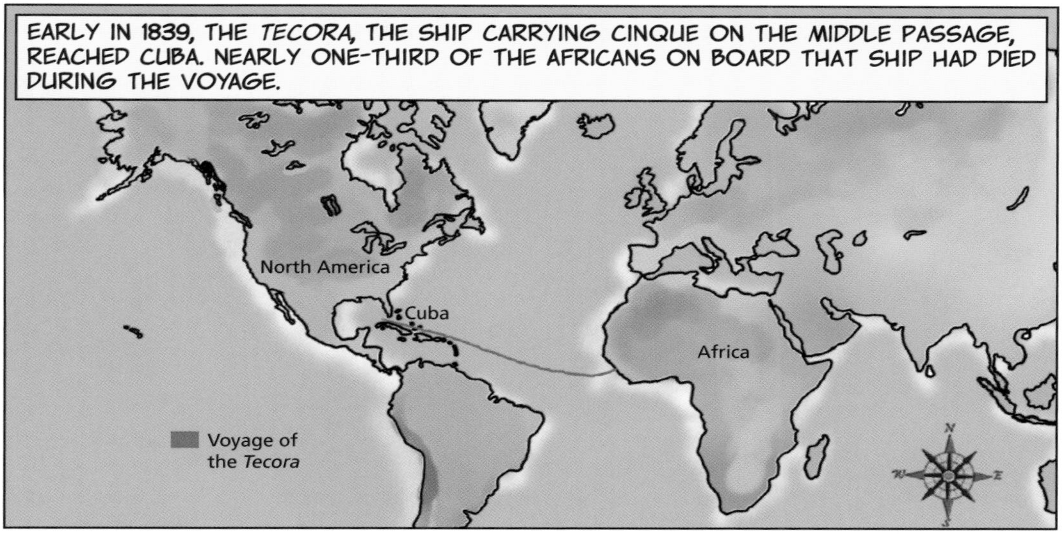
EARLY IN 1839, THE *TECORA*, THE SHIP CARRYING CINQUE ON THE MIDDLE PASSAGE, REACHED CUBA. NEARLY ONE-THIRD OF THE AFRICANS ON BOARD THAT SHIP HAD DIED DURING THE VOYAGE.
North America
Cuba
Africa
Voyage of the *Tecora*
N
W
E
S

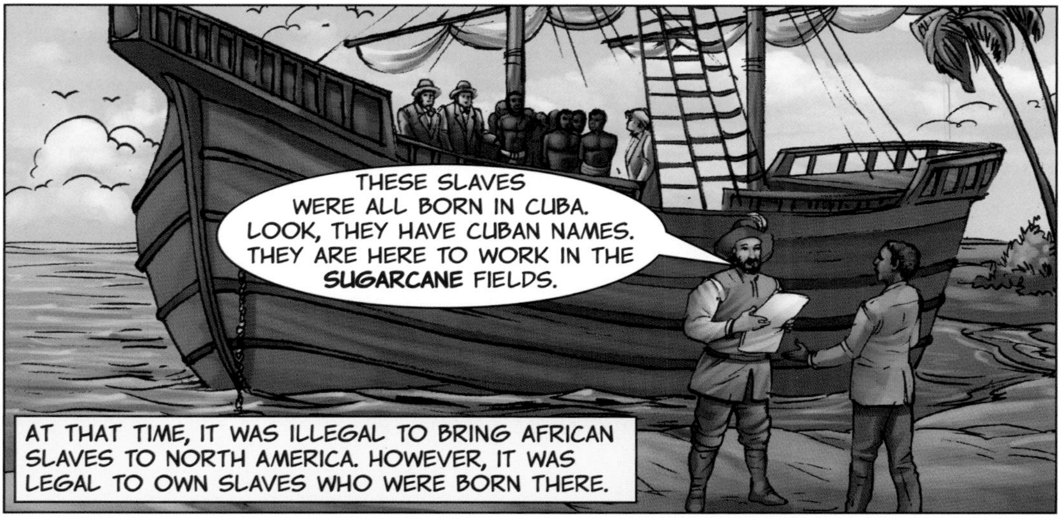
THESE SLAVES WERE ALL BORN IN CUBA. LOOK, THEY HAVE CUBAN NAMES. THEY ARE HERE TO WORK IN THE **SUGARCANE** FIELDS.
AT THAT TIME, IT WAS ILLEGAL TO BRING AFRICAN SLAVES TO NORTH AMERICA. HOWEVER, IT WAS LEGAL TO OWN SLAVES WHO WERE BORN THERE.

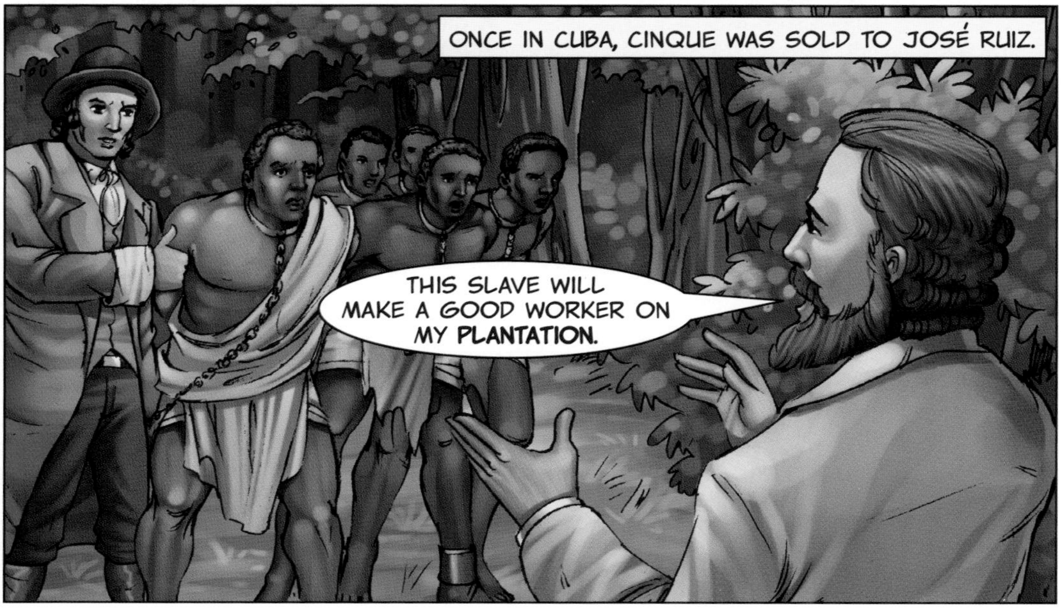
ONCE IN CUBA, CINQUE WAS SOLD TO JOSÉ RUIZ.
THIS SLAVE WILL MAKE A GOOD WORKER ON MY **PLANTATION**.

ALONG WITH 48 OTHER AFRICAN MEN, CINQUE WAS LOADED ONTO A SHIP NAMED THE *AMISTAD*.

WHILE BOUND BELOW THE SHIP'S DECK, CINQUE FOUND A BENT NAIL. HE USED IT TO UNDO HIS METAL COLLAR.

I THINK I MIGHT BE ABLE TO GET FREE.

CINQUE QUICKLY FREED THE OTHERS.

WE CAN TAKE OVER THE SHIP. WE WILL GO BACK TO AFRICA.

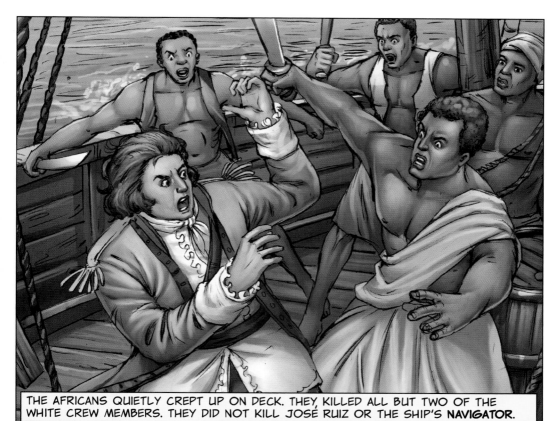

THE AFRICANS QUIETLY CREPT UP ON DECK. THEY KILLED ALL BUT TWO OF THE WHITE CREW MEMBERS. THEY DID NOT KILL JOSÉ RUIZ OR THE SHIP'S **NAVIGATOR**.

CINQUE FORCED THE NAVIGATOR TO SAIL THE SHIP EAST, TOWARD THE RISING SUN, BECAUSE HE KNEW THAT WAS THE DIRECTION OF HIS HOMELAND.

THE NAVIGATOR SAILED EAST DURING THE DAY, BUT HE TRICKED THE AFRICANS. AT NIGHT, USING THE STARS FOR DIRECTION, HE SAILED NORTH AND WEST. HE WANTED TO GET TO THE UNITED STATES. GRADUALLY, THE SHIP WORKED ITS WAY UP THE COAST OF THE UNITED STATES.

IN AUGUST 1839, THE UNITED STATES NAVY STOPPED THE SHIP. BECAUSE THE AFRICANS DID NOT SPEAK ENGLISH, THE NAVAL CAPTAIN COULD NOT TALK WITH THEM.

WE ARE GOING TO **TOW** THIS SHIP TO SHORE.

THE *AMISTAD* WAS TOWED TO NEW LONDON, CONNECTICUT.

ONCE ON SHORE, THE AFRICANS WERE PUT IN JAIL. OFFICIALS SAID THEY HAD MURDERED THE *AMISTAD'S* CREW. THEY ALSO SAID THE AFRICANS HAD STOLEN THE SHIP.

WHAT WILL BECOME OF US?

WE WILL FIGHT FOR OUR FREEDOM HOWEVER WE CAN.

THERE WERE MANY PEOPLE IN THE AREA WHO THOUGHT SLAVERY WAS WRONG. THEY WERE KNOWN AS ABOLITIONISTS.

DID YOU HEAR ABOUT THE AFRICANS WHO TOOK OVER A SLAVE SHIP? THEY ARE NOW IN JAIL.

WE MUST HELP THEM. NO ONE SHOULD BE FORCED INTO SLAVERY!

13

IF THE AFRICANS HAD BEEN BORN IN CUBA, THEY WOULD HAVE SPOKEN SPANISH. THEY DID NOT. CINQUE SPOKE AN AFRICAN LANGUAGE KNOWN AS MENDE.

THE ABOLITIONISTS STARTED THE *AMISTAD* COMMITTEE.

WE WILL FIND A WAY TO FREE THESE AFRICANS.

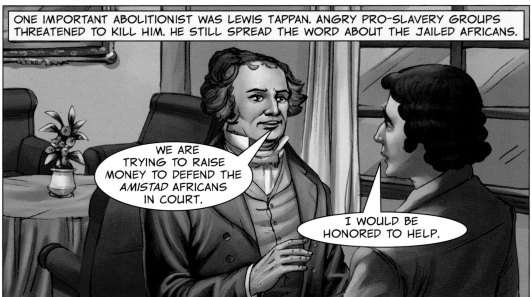

ONE IMPORTANT ABOLITIONIST WAS LEWIS TAPPAN. ANGRY PRO-SLAVERY GROUPS THREATENED TO KILL HIM. HE STILL SPREAD THE WORD ABOUT THE JAILED AFRICANS.

WE ARE TRYING TO RAISE MONEY TO DEFEND THE *AMISTAD* AFRICANS IN COURT.

I WOULD BE HONORED TO HELP.

THE *AMISTAD* COMMITTEE WAS ABLE TO FIND A FREE BLACK MAN WHO KNEW CINQUE'S LANGUAGE. HE COULD TRANSLATE CINQUE'S WORDS INTO ENGLISH.

TELL ME, HOW DID YOU GET HERE?

I WAS CAPTURED FROM MY HOMELAND AND BROUGHT HERE ON A SHIP.

THE **TRANSLATOR** LEARNED THAT THE SLAVE TRADERS HAD ILLEGALLY BROUGHT THESE SLAVES TO CUBA.

WE WERE SOLD AS SLAVES AND WERE BEING SENT TO ANOTHER PLANTATION TO WORK. MAYBE THEY WERE GOING TO KILL US, SO WE TOOK OVER THE SHIP.

AT THIS TIME, MARTIN VAN BUREN WAS PRESIDENT OF THE UNITED STATES. CUBA BELONGED TO SPAIN. THE SPANISH GOVERNMENT TOLD THE PRESIDENT THAT THE AFRICANS WERE THE PROPERTY OF SPAIN.

THESE SLAVES WERE BORN IN CUBA. THIS MEANS THEY BELONG TO SPAIN.

YOU KNOW THAT THOSE PAPERS ARE **FRAUDULENT**. THESE PEOPLE WERE TAKEN ILLEGALLY FROM THEIR HOMES IN AFRICA.

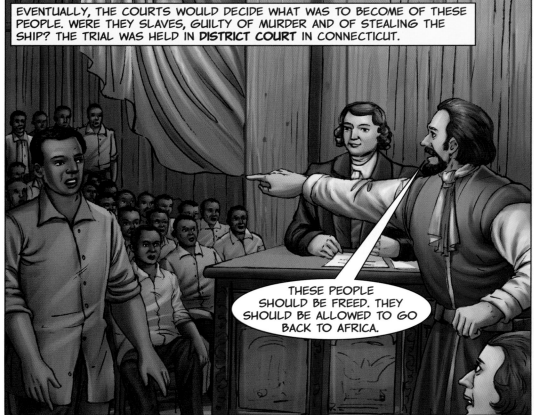

EVENTUALLY, THE COURTS WOULD DECIDE WHAT WAS TO BECOME OF THESE PEOPLE. WERE THEY SLAVES, GUILTY OF MURDER AND OF STEALING THE SHIP? THE TRIAL WAS HELD IN **DISTRICT COURT** IN CONNECTICUT.

THESE PEOPLE SHOULD BE FREED. THEY SHOULD BE ALLOWED TO GO BACK TO AFRICA.

THE JUDGE AGREED WITH THE LAWYER.

SPAIN DOES NOT OWN THESE AFRICANS. I ORDER THAT THESE PEOPLE BE SET FREE IMMEDIATELY.

PRESIDENT VAN BUREN DISAGREED WITH THE JUDGE'S DECISION. HE SAID THAT THE UNITED STATES SUPREME COURT SHOULD HEAR THE CASE.

I AM ORDERING THAT THIS CASE BE DECIDED BY THE SUPREME COURT.

THE *AMISTAD* COMMITTEE ASKED JOHN QUINCY ADAMS TO HELP THE AFRICANS. HE HAD SERVED AS PRESIDENT OF THE UNITED STATES FROM 1825 TO 1829.

THE SUPREME COURT IS GOING TO HEAR THE CASE.

I WILL BE THE AFRICANS' LAWYER. I DON'T LIKE SLAVERY, AND I WANT TO SEE JUSTICE DONE HERE.

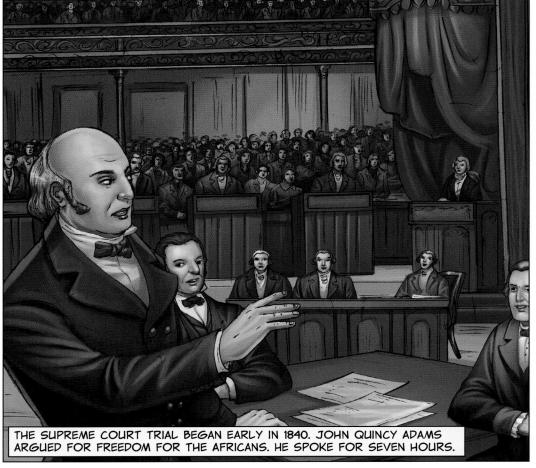

THE SUPREME COURT TRIAL BEGAN EARLY IN 1840. JOHN QUINCY ADAMS ARGUED FOR FREEDOM FOR THE AFRICANS. HE SPOKE FOR SEVEN HOURS.

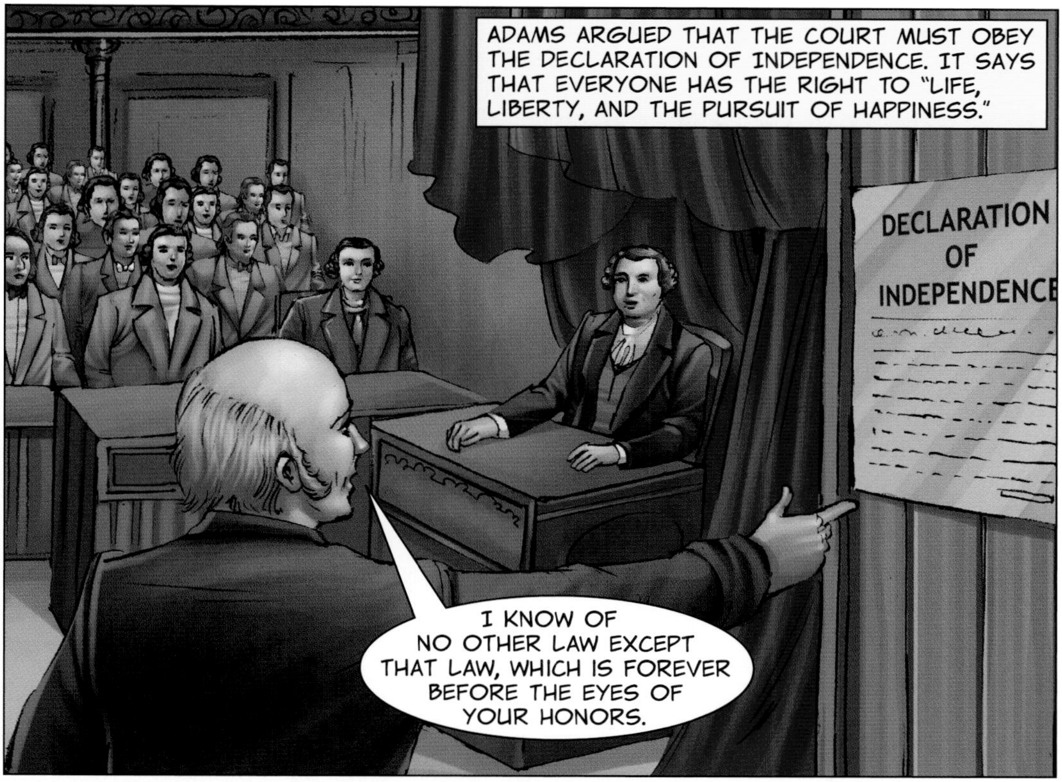
ADAMS ARGUED THAT THE COURT MUST OBEY THE DECLARATION OF INDEPENDENCE. IT SAYS THAT EVERYONE HAS THE RIGHT TO "LIFE, LIBERTY, AND THE PURSUIT OF HAPPINESS."
DECLARATION OF INDEPENDENCE
I KNOW OF NO OTHER LAW EXCEPT THAT LAW, WHICH IS FOREVER BEFORE THE EYES OF YOUR HONORS.

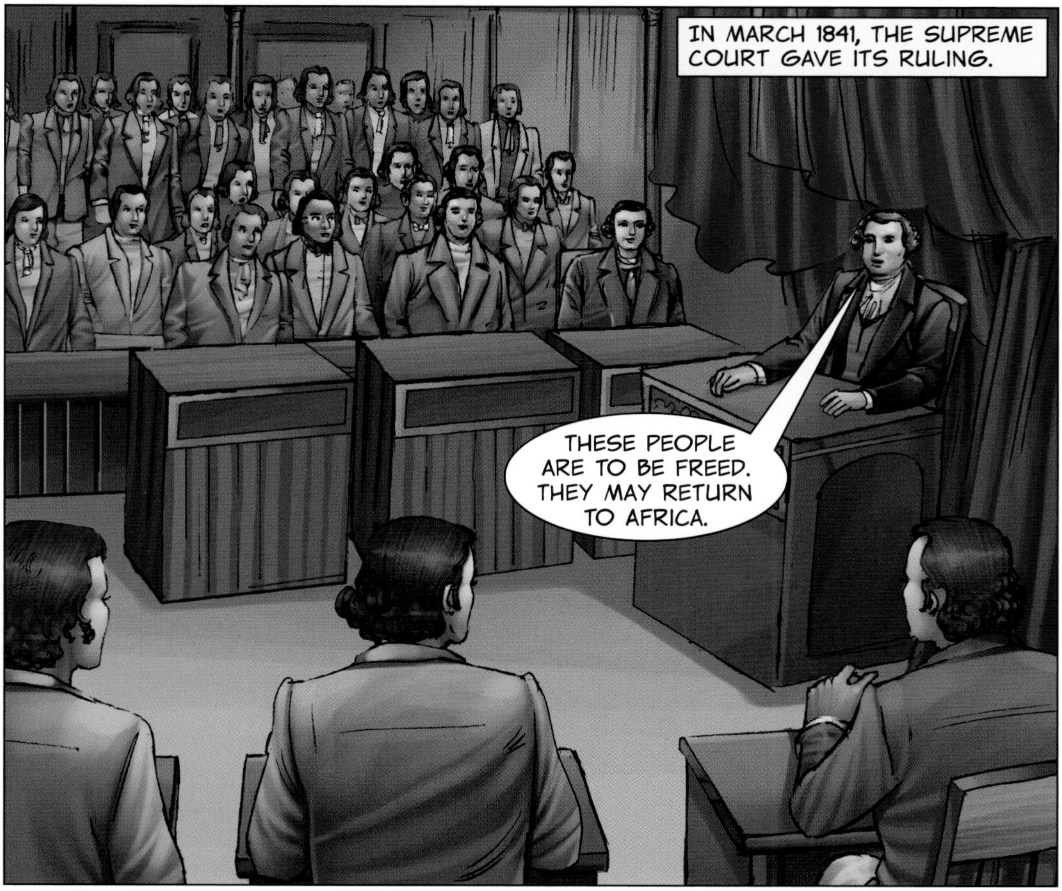
IN MARCH 1841, THE SUPREME COURT GAVE ITS RULING.
THESE PEOPLE ARE TO BE FREED. THEY MAY RETURN TO AFRICA.

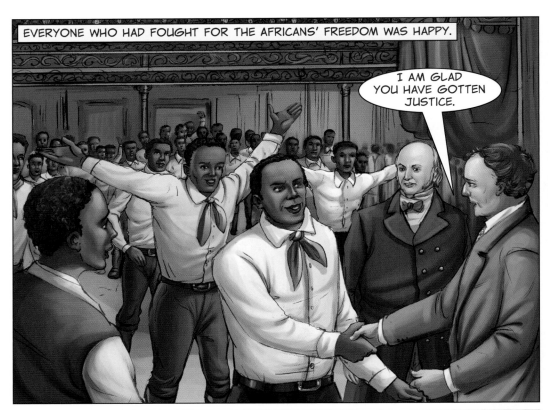

EVERYONE WHO HAD FOUGHT FOR THE AFRICANS' FREEDOM WAS HAPPY.

I AM GLAD YOU HAVE GOTTEN JUSTICE.

THE UNITED STATES GOVERNMENT WOULD NOT PAY FOR THE AFRICANS TO GO HOME. SO THE ABOLITIONISTS RAISED THE MONEY.

WILL YOU GIVE MONEY SO THE AFRICANS CAN GET BACK TO THEIR HOMELAND?

NEAR THE END OF 1841, 35 SURVIVORS OF THE *AMISTAD* WENT BACK TO AFRICA. SEVERAL WHITE MINISTERS AND THEIR FAMILIES WENT WITH THEM. SOME OF THEM SET UP A **MISSION**. THEY WORKED TO HELP IMPROVE PEOPLE'S LIVES.

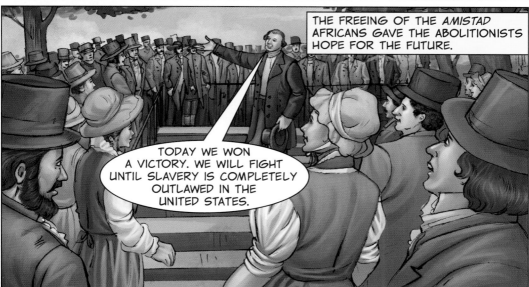

THE FREEING OF THE *AMISTAD* AFRICANS GAVE THE ABOLITIONISTS HOPE FOR THE FUTURE.

TODAY WE WON A VICTORY. WE WILL FIGHT UNTIL SLAVERY IS COMPLETELY OUTLAWED IN THE UNITED STATES.

THIS ONE SMALL GROUP OF AFRICANS ESCAPED SLAVERY AND EARNED A PLACE IN HISTORY. HOWEVER, LARGE NUMBERS OF AFRICANS DIED DURING THE MIDDLE PASSAGE.

UNTIL THE END OF THE CIVIL WAR, THOUSANDS OF OTHER AFRICANS AND THEIR DESCENDANTS ENDURED THE HORRORS OF BEING ENSLAVED. FINALLY, IN DECEMBER 1865, THE THIRTEENTH AMENDMENT WAS RATIFIED. THAT AMENDMENT BANNED SLAVERY FOREVER THROUGHOUT THE UNITED STATES.

Timeline

1619	First African slaves are brought to North American colonies.
c. 1814	Cinque is born in Mendeland, which was near Sierra Leone.
January 1839	Cinque, along with several hundred others, is captured. They are sold into slavery.
April 1839	Cinque and his fellow enslaved Africans begin their voyage to Cuba.
Late June 1839	The *Amistad* sets sail from Havana to Puerto Principe, Cuba, with the enslaved Africans on board.
Early July 1839	Cinque and his fellow African captives take over the *Amistad*.
August 1839	The *Amistad* is captured by U.S. authorities, and the Africans are jailed.
January 1840	The Connecticut District Court rules the Africans should be freed.
February 1840	President Van Buren states that the United States Supreme Court should hear the case.
February 1841	Former President John Quincy Adams argues for the Africans before the Supreme Court.
March 1841	The Supreme Court says the Africans are free and may return to their homeland.
November 1841	Cinque and his fellow Africans board a ship to return to Africa. They are accompanied by white **missionaries**.
January 1842	Cinque, his fellow Africans, and the white missionaries reach Sierra Leone.

Glossary

abolitionist (a-buh-LIH-shun-ist) A person who worked to end slavery.

captors (KAP-turz) People who take control by force.

defended (dih-FEND-ed) Took someone's side in an argument.

district court (DIS-trikt KORT) The place in a particular region where people who break rules or laws are judged.

fraudulent (FROD-joo-lent) Using lies or tricks to cheat or to take advantage of a situation in a way that is against the law.

hygiene (HY-jeen) Things that you do in order to stay healthy by keeping yourself and things around you clean.

mission (MIH-shun) A place where church leaders teach their beliefs and help the community.

missionaries (MIH-shuh-ner-eez) A group of people sent to a foreign country to teach people about a certain religion.

navigator (NA-vuh-gay-ter) A person who uses maps, the stars, or special tools to travel in a ship, an aircraft, or a rocket.

plantation (plan-TAY-shun) A very large farm where crops are grown.

profitable (PRAH-fih-tuh-buhl) Giving wealth or profit.

sugarcane (SHUH-gur-kayn) A type of grass that has sugar juice in its stems.

tow (TOH) To haul or to pull along.

translator (trans-LAY-ter) A person who helps people who speak different languages understand each other.

Triangular Trade (try-AN-gyoo-lur TRAYD) Merchant trade between the New World, Europe, and Africa.

Index

A

abolitionists, 3, 13, 14, 20, 21
Adams, John Quincy, 3, 18, 19
Africa, 3, 5, 9, 10, 14, 16, 19, 21
Amistad, 3, 6, 10, 12, 13, 21
Amistad committee, 14, 15, 18
Atlantic Ocean, 3, 8

C

Cinque, 3, 7, 9, 10, 11, 14, 15
Civil War, 21
Cuba, 3, 9, 12, 14, 15, 16

D

Declaration of Independence, 19

E

Europe, 5, 6

H

Havana, Cuba, 3

M

Mendeland, 7
Mende language, 14
Middle Passage, 3, 5, 6, 9, 21

N

New London, Connecticut, 12

P

Puerto Principe, Cuba, 3

R

Ruiz, José, 3, 9, 11

S

Sierra Leone, 7, 12
Spain, 16, 17

T

Tappan, Lewis, 3, 14
Tecora, 9, 12
Thirteenth Amendment, 21
Triangular Trade, 5, 6

U

United States Navy, 12
United States Supreme Court,
   17, 18, 19

V

Van Buren, Martin, 3, 16, 17

W

West Africa, 4, 7

Websites

Due to the changing nature of Internet links, PowerKids Press has developed an online list of websites related to the subject of this book. This site is updated regularly. Please use this link to access the list:

www.powerkidslinks.com/jgaah/revolt/